FUTURE COMPUTER 2023

Modern Poetry

Paula Glynn

What It Is Like To Fly On An Airplane

When boarding the modern aircraft
You feel a sense of soul crushing fear
Yet crucial heart beating excitement
You knowing you're bravely flying
High in that glorious blue sky
At 35, 000 thousand feet
Your face at first as white as a sheet

Sitting in your comfortable airplane seat
You watch the other passengers board
No one on the airplane ignored
No one on the airplane bored
Because air travel is yours
And an important part of your working life
Whether you are flying daily or yearly

The airplane taxis up the runway
Slow at first but soon speeding up
Its wings lifted from air above
The wings soaring passengers
Through quickly increasing altitude
Into and through the blue sky at 700 MPH
Passengers being sold food and soft drinks

The downside being turbulence
The airplane hitting uncooperative air
Some people on board not to care
But other passengers very aware
And wondering if they need to beware
But soon the flight turns to normal
Passengers no longer feeling anxiety

Short hours to long hours spent flying
Every airplane ride different

Destinations all across the world
Destinations taking people everywhere
The airplane not designed to scare
Because advanced technology has
Made the aviation industry aware

That air travel must be safe
And have strict protocols
Every pilot highly advanced
Vastly skilled and deeply respected
Keeping every trip safe for passengers
In fact, safer than driving
Airplane travel easy with nothing to fear
Instead excitement and happiness here.

Aquarius

The star sign Aquarius element of air
The symbol of water bearer
Ruling planet Uranus: with its predictable personality traits
Birth stones Amazing Amethyst and Gorgeous Garnet
Opulent Opal, Sexy Sugilite,
Jolly Jasper and Magical Moss Agate
Artistic Aquarius to innovate and create
A personality with one to always relate
Articulate Aquarius quirky aspects
Personality traits from January 19 to February 18.

Aquarius most innovative and progressive
Rebellious and goal inspired humanitarian
Aquarius often found planning a revolution
Proudly flaunting their funky fashion sensibility
Having an often overlooked sensitive side
Requiring appreciation, support and love
Their heart true like an angel from above
But also having heartfelt and positive pride
That keeps good luck on their side.

Aquarius air energy all about the mind
About every emotional Zodiac star sign
Being incredibly intellectual and deeply social
Curiosity the common trait
With an Aquarius: make no mistake
When it comes to interpersonal dynamics
No one to change this air sign or shake

Sense into: common sense already there
The regular Aquarius to do as they dare.

Myth of Aquarius: representation of being grounded
A larger-than-life, mythical being
One foot firmly planted on the fertile soil
One foot positioned in the wayward water
As Aquarius pours a vase of inspiration
To cultivate longevity, healing, and hope
This Zodiac sign offering vision that does scope
For Aquarius being a lucky air sign to be born to
For Aquarius being a unique star sign to be born to.

Spaceman X

The first view of blue and green earth in orbit
Dreaming of travelling through the universe
Spaceman X feels tremendous excitement
Knowing that his highly advanced spaceship
Is finally taking him through
The mysterious and strange universe

The spaceship has its clocks
Continue running through
Universe space and time
The echoes of dark matter
The echoes of dark energy
Telling the story of the universe

To see the universe back in time
When all matter was condensed unto one
When the energy of strange something
Decided it would expand beyond imagination
And create galaxies and stars and planets
And eventually creating life-giving earth

Spaceman X having learnt from textbooks
Then learning to fly airplanes
Then learning to fly spaceships
His pilot expertise and experience incredible
His qualifications and practice invaluable
His knowledge and intelligence protecting lives

Leaving earth's atmosphere and orbit
Spaceman X navigates up, down, left and right

The directions of space travel four dimensional
While travelling through the solar system
Spaceman X passes by Jupiter, Mars
Venus, Saturn, other planets and hostile moons

With no agenda to land on these impossible
Planets and moons: temperature and gravity
That would destroy any spaceship
That tried to land: gravity to completely crush
No human spaceship to make that mistake
Where planets and moons even aliens would avoid

Light years pass: nothing faster than light
Not even a spaceship even fast enough
Spaceman X having it tough
Knowing auto-pilot not a good idea
At least when he doesn't sleep
In a specially designed space bed

Spaceman X to often miss days and nights
But he always knew when that airplane
Soared into the air, taking flight
Space travel for him was right
His heart's desire to explore the universe
And to be like a character on Star Trek

Still: sometimes Spaceman X
Would long for a cup of coffee in the morning
And a cup of tea in the afternoon
And to feel the grass under his feet
And feel the summer sun on his face
That sacrifice he made to advance the human race

Although fiction, Star Trek to amaze audiences
And to inspire a new generation
To take to the stellar skies
To be spaceman X that flies
Through the hostile vacuum of outer space
And live a life that is trip the light fantastic.

Mission To Mars

A NASA spaceship travelling to Mars
With scientific studies from 1940
Humans wishing to explore the red planet

Its mysteries beyond NASA landing on the moon
Like a fairytale of a hungry bear and porridge on a spoon
Space technology advancing the human race all too soon

Proposals imagining the human mission to Mars:
Robotic Landers and rovers testing the ecology of the red planet
2022 the year of the NASA space age
Humans travelling to Mars central stage
Multiple organizations planning the journey
A long three month journey through space

NASA's billion dollar project to never lose face:
For Mars is a planet that could take earth's place
At least in fantasy: the Martians actually human
But will there be conflict between earth and Mars?
Will the human race travel beyond the solar system?
Will humans invade space and travel quickly and far?

Many plans made for space exploration:
Perhaps a crew of eight astronauts
Staying for a month or so
Staying in their research stations,
Even colonization and continuous habitation
The red planet the second home of the human race

The media excited about the mission to Mars
Ever since it discovered by astronomers
Science fiction written about the red planet
Throughout three centuries of people only knowing fantasy
For Mars shall be the new earth
A place where people travelling through space don't have to search

People travelling to Mars on commercial trips
Living in a spaceship for three long months
Having previously had space tests and practices
Seeing if passengers able to cope with lack of gravity
Travelling in space different to an airplane
Some people believing those space explorers insane

But they are not insane: their adventures
Shall take them to the red planet for two months
A space adventure having just begun
For the human race sees beyond the sun
And sees the earth spinning in orbit:
An image beyond exciting and wonderful

Once having landed on Mars
And having quarters on Mars buildings
It is time to explore on a buggy:
Mars terrain similar to earth grit and rocks
Passengers on the buggy for hours
The sun as hot as the sun shining onto a beach

There are rules: no drugs, alcohol or cigarettes
There is no violence and the medical services excellent
These red planet explorers also having been vetted
Before their three month journey through space
Brave and strong people they are
Knowing the dangers and risks of their adventure

Every "Sunday" on the red planet Skype is used
Family and friends back home excitedly
Asking about their Mars adventure
The media also all over this Mission To Mars
Major Internet newspapers boasting about NASA
In their computer generated headlines

The spaceship pilots to take many loads of people -
Regular people - to and from the red planet
The holiday that exhilarating and fantastic
Many passengers confident when leaving
Earth's atmosphere and entering Martian gravity
Gravity measured differently on Mars

Many poems and short stories written about Mars:
But for a reason: Mars belongs to earth
Future humans living and breathing on Mars
Future humans feeding themselves and expanding
On that once mysterious red planet
Because Mars has shown the human race will live forever.

I Used To Be Guanlong

The first cut is the deepest
I started out as Guanlong
In the depths of historical time
Millions and millions of years
The earth older than ever realized

I walked the earth 75kg
Light for a dinosaur

Yet I did hunt in packs
Yet I did have powerful jaws
And legs that could run incredibly fast

Geological changes forced
Me to flee the vicious south
For the nature rich north
Grass and trees and fields
Waiting for me: a tiny T-Rex to roam

Volcanoes to explode
During the Jurassic period
Forcing every dinosaur to flee
The terrain too hot and too brutal
To even consider staying living on

Continuing the predator hunt
As millions of years go past
My once light Guanlong body
Now weighing 6000kg:
Six tons of sheer brutal force

My jaws could brutally crush
Another dinosaur's neck in seconds
My fierce roar having every dinosaur
Running in terrible and life preserving fear
No dinosaur wanting me anywhere near

I am the message of evolution:
Going from small and weak
To gradually becoming loud
Powerful and reigning supreme
Loving every dinosaur scream

My bird brain designed to hunt
To plan the attack and kill in a pack
To camouflage in the dense trees
Wanting an easy target to kill
Getting an instinctual thrill of the hunt

However I can't run for too long:
My bones could break
And my heart could burst
And going without food for too long
Makes me weak and slow

Ultimately I am a fierce predator
I am the king of the dinosaur world
I am the symbol of ultimate fear
Yet maybe I can eat the slaves
And free the innocent from their fear.

The Indian Princess And Her Tiger

The Indian Princess walks her tiger
Around the opulent palace grounds
Her strong tiger always serving and obeying her
Every utterance and command she does vocalize
For her tiger is her ultimate protection.

The Indian Princess grew up with her pet tiger:
She knew he was safe to always be around
And the Indian princess is protected
By his true animal grace
That no other animal could ever replace.

The Indian princess grooms her tiger
Gently with a special comb
Her tiger also loving to groom himself:
His coat striped orange and black
A tiger no one to kill or attack.

The Indian Princess loves her pet tiger
Whilst others fear him
For the Indian princess's tiger does have stealth
And a fierce roar heard all over the palace
Her enemies knowing to stay far away.

The Indian princess does feed her pet tiger:
All kinds of especially prepared raw meat
With many pieces of meat her tiger needs
Because he is her royal protection
And if anyone attacks her, they will bleed.

The Indian princess cherishes
Her beautiful and magnificent tiger
For her animal will never perish
At the hands of a dangerous gun
Only her pet orange and black tiger having won.

The Indian princess shall always remember

That powerful and athletic pet tiger
Because her gorgeous tiger protected her
And warned her enemies to not get too close
They not wanting to be mauled.

The Indian princess never to replace her pet tiger
Having loved bathing with him in the small pool
Having run with him across the vast palace grounds
Having hidden cat treats that her tiger found
Having an animal with compassion and strength.

The Indian princess feeling proud
Every curious person getting excited and loud
The circus show in the vast and excited crowd
Gasping in awe at the Princess' tiger doing its rounds
The stage man showcasing a roar that is strong and loud.

The Indian princess taking her tiger
Off that colourful and traditional circus stage
But after the tiger tamer doing his performance not into a metal cage
Because although her tiger can attack and feel rage
That is not happening: at least not today.

The Indian princess seeing her protective tiger
Inevitably grow into old age
The Indian princess glad he was never kept in a restricting cage
For the Indian princess loves her deceased from age tiger
A tiger with an old and wise soul and with a true heart.

The Lipstick Story: Italian Translation

La storia del rossetto: The History Of Lipstick

Il rossetto ha una lunga storia,
Le donne nell'antica civiltà della Valle,
Chicchi di caffè schiacciati e applicati alle labbra,
Rossetto sulle labbra per decorazione e fascino antico,
Gli Egiziani prendendo colorante rosso violaceo,
Da coleotteri e formiche per base,
Rossetto anche gli antichi decorano per il loro viso.

L'età dell'oro islamica,
Il noto cosmetologo arabo andaluso,
Abu al-Qasim al-Zahrawi,
Inventando il rossetto solido,

Ceppi profumati laminati e pressati in stampi,
Questo lo descrive come Al-Tasrif,
Perché anche allora,
Le donne sono considerate belle e affascinanti,
Rossetto lo sguardo migliaia di anni fa.

Nell'Europa medievale, la chiesa in armi,
Vietare il rossetto, perché il rossetto era,
L'incarnazione di Satana,
Quel proiettile colorato è opera del diavolo,
Donne evitate dalla società,
Per aver osato colorare le loro labbra,
Ma il tempo passò e il XVI secolo,
Ha permesso alle donne di dipingere le loro labbra,
Il regno di Elisabetta I,
Facendo labbra rosse e facce bianche,
Una dichiarazione di moda,
E il permesso per le donne,
Per celebrare la loro bellezza con il rossetto,
Rossetto ora fatto di cera d'api,
E macchie rosse dalle piante,
Lo scarabeo schiacciato non è più utilizzato.

Il rossetto della seconda guerra mondiale ha guadagnato popolarità,
La pubblicità dell'industria cinematografica,
Il rossetto rosso delle stelle,
Attrici e figure glamour irraggiungibili,
Con i loro vestiti alla moda e costosi,
Che le donne che lavorano potrebbero mal permettersi,
E le labbra imbronciate mentre applicavano il rossetto,
Ma le donne inferiori comprerebbero rossetti lussureggianti,
E guarda nello specchio,
Sapendo che ha l'aspetto delle stelle,
Inizia una tradizione dell'industria della moda.

Molte donne lavoratrici chiamavano il rossetto rossetto,
Rossetto paragonato a una donna che vuole amore,
Perché il rossetto rosso è il colore della passione,
Non solo il colore scelto per la moda,
La frase "Mettere il rossetto su un maiale"
Entrando in gioco, significato,
Per rendere ciò che è poco attraente superficialmente attraente,
E, naturalmente, c'è il rossetto lesbico,
Termine non troppo dispregiativo,
Ma molte donne indossano il rossetto,
I loro antenati portano la tendenza,

Il rossetto sta diventando un'accettazione rocciosa,
Perché questa è la storia del rossetto,
Dove le donne possono ora godere,
Rossetti di molti colori,
Ogni colore della pelle e ogni bocca,
Catering per, glamour e bellezza,
Il massimo della vita moderna.

The Lipstick Story: Direct Translation From Italian

Lipstick has a long history,
Women in the ancient civilization of the Valley,
Coffee beans crushed and applied to the lips,
Lipstick on the lips for decoration and old-fashioned charm,
The Egyptians taking purplish-red dye,
From beetles and ants to base,
Lipstick even the ancients decorate for their face.

The Islamic Golden Age,
The well-known Arab Andalusian cosmetologist,
Abu al-Qasim al-Zahrawi,
Inventing solid lipstick,
Scented logs rolled and pressed into moulds,
This describes him as Al-Tasrif,
Because even then,
Women are considered beautiful and charming,
Lipstick looked thousands of years ago.

In medieval Europe, the church in arms,
Ban lipstick, because lipstick was,
The incarnation of Satan,
That colored bullet is the work of the devil,
women shunned by society,
For daring to color their lips,
But time passed and the sixteenth century,
He allowed women to paint their lips,
The reign of Elizabeth I,
Making red lips and white faces,
A fashion statement,
And permission for women,
To celebrate their beauty with lipstick,
Lipstick now made of beeswax,
And red spots from the plants,
The squashed beetle is no longer used.

WWII lipstick gained popularity,
Film industry advertising,
The red lipstick of the stars,
Unreachable actresses and glamorous figures,
With their fashionable and expensive clothes,
That working women could ill afford,
And the lips pouted as they applied the lipstick,
But inferior women would buy lush lipsticks,
And look in the mirror,
Knowing that it looks like stars,
Start a tradition of the fashion industry.

Many working women called lipstick lipstick,
Lipstick compared to a woman who wants love,
Because red lipstick is the color of passion,
Not only the color chosen for fashion,
The phrase "Put lipstick on a pig"
Coming into play, meaning,
To make the unattractive superficially attractive,
And, of course, there's the lesbian lipstick,
Not too derogatory term
But many women wear lipstick,
Their ancestors lead the trend,
Lipstick is becoming a rocky acceptance,
Because this is the story of lipstick,
Where women can now enjoy,
Lipsticks of many colors,
Every skin color and every mouth,
Catering for, glamor and beauty,
The pinnacle of modern living.

The Lipstick Story: In Spanish

la historia del pintalabios

El lápiz labial tiene una larga historia,
Mujeres en la antigua Civilización del Valle,
Granos de café triturados y aplicados a los labios,
Pintalabios en labios para decoración y glamour antiguo,
Los egipcios tomando tinte rojo púrpura,
De escarabajos y hormigas para la base,
Barra de labios que incluso los antiguos decoran para su rostro.

La edad de oro islámica,
La notable cosmetóloga árabe andaluza,

Abu al-Qasim al-Zahrawi,
Inventando el lápiz labial sólido,
Cepas perfumadas laminadas y prensadas en moldes,
Esto lo describe como Al-Tasrif,
Porque incluso entonces,
Las mujeres son consideradas hermosas y glamorosas,
Pintalabios el look de hace miles de años.

En la Europa medieval, la iglesia levantada en armas,
Prohibir el lápiz labial, porque el lápiz labial era,
La Encarnación de Satanás,
Esa bala de colores obra del diablo,
Mujeres rechazadas por la sociedad,
por atreverse a colorear sus labios,
Pero pasó el tiempo y el siglo XVI,
Permitió que las mujeres se pintaran los labios,
El reinado de Isabel I,
Haciendo labios rojos y caras blancas,
Una declaración de moda,
Y permiso para las mujeres,
Para celebrar su belleza con pintalabios,
Lápiz labial ahora hecho de cera de abejas,
y las manchas rojas de las plantas,
El escarabajo aplastado ya no se usa.

El lápiz labial de la Segunda Guerra Mundial ganó popularidad,
La publicidad de la industria del cine,
El labial rojo de las estrellas,
Actrices y figuras de glamour inalcanzables,
Con su ropa de moda y cara,
que las mujeres trabajadoras no podían permitirse,
Y los labios haciendo pucheros mientras se aplicaban el pintalabios,
Pero las mujeres menores comprarían lápiz labial exuberante,
y mirarme al espejo,
Sabiendo que tiene el aspecto de las estrellas,
Comenzó una tradición de la industria de la moda.

Muchas mujeres trabajadoras se referían al lápiz labial como lippy,
Lápiz labial comparado con una mujer que quiere amor,
Porque el lápiz labial rojo es el color de la pasión,
No solo el color elegido para la moda,
La frase 'Poner lápiz labial en un cerdo'
Entrar en juego, es decir,
Para hacer lo poco atractivo superficialmente atractivo,
Y, por supuesto, está la lesbiana pintalabios,
Un término no demasiado despectivo,

Pero muchas mujeres usan lápiz labial,
Sus ancestros llevando la tendencia,
Lápiz labial entrando en aceptación rocosa,
Porque esta es la historia del lápiz labial,
Donde las mujeres ahora pueden disfrutar,
Barras de labios de muchos colores,
Cada color de piel y cada boca,
Atendido, glamour y belleza,
Lo último en la vida moderna.

Hospital Nightshift

It is wintertime and the cold night falls
At 4:30 in the afternoon as predicted
Where the city of London comes alive
Many attractive young men and women
Enjoying their vivacious and vibrant nightlife
That explodes with the pulse of popularity

The important ambulance service
And the local London hospital
Waiting for all those night-time dramas
Where young men get into fierce fights
Where young women totter on their high heels
The night full of drugs and alcohol intoxication

Where problems with paradise do reveal
And the once happy neon night
Drugs and alcohol do selfishly steal
But the hospital nightshift workers
Makes enthusiastic club goers
Realize it is probably time to go home to bed

But some to spend night-time
In the busy hospital ward
Where they fall asleep restfully
And by the nightshift staff are not ignored
And never show if they've had enough
Their hard work taking patients to the morning

Time never stopping and time predictable
Time a constant: especially in the hospital
The range of emergencies
And the range of injuries and health issues
Do keep night staff constantly busy

Their time spent keeping the public safe

Gratitude to be given to those
Hard working hospital staff: daytime and nightshift
Staff that save lives and keeps the city safer
Nightshift staff going on duty night-after-night
Club - and even restaurant and public house goers -
Able to wake to another cold London morning.

Just Another Sip Of My Margarita

I flew into glamorous Lanzarote
Sipping my sweet and refreshing margarita
Enjoying the dry and desolate hot sun
My old aggressors having not won

I am wearing my yellow bikini beside the blue sea
I love the sun's hot rays pouring down on me
I love the free people wandering around
No one upset or angry or wearing a frown

I eat at night in luxurious restaurants
Lanzarote food and drink delicious
I sleep with the breeze from the refreshing open window
Not worried about bugs getting in

I feel as if I am living in an unreal dream
And a deeply happy dream it is too
And I am glad not to be the ugly you
Still I am only here for another week

So I take another sip of my margarita
Wishing time would magically slow down
And I wouldn't be back in cold London next week
Wearing your monotonous frown.

Whispers From The Corner Of The Room

The room is pitch black
No light from the moon
The day in the prison done
Dreaded tomorrow morning waiting
To follow the same dull chores
Principles and approach

Needing to assume a fake identity

And he lays in his isolated prison cell
His bed as hard as hell
Because his life is far from swell
His once sweet tooth
Now as bitter as hell
Smoking those lung cancer cigarettes instead
For he cries every night in his prison bed

But one night in the darkness
He hears a whisper
"Are you alone?"
Surprised "Yes, who are you?"
"I'm above you, in the corner of the room."
And sure enough a spider appears
Seemingly seeing him in the darkness

And a beautiful spider too:
With a blue and white striped body
Supernatural green eyes glowing wonder
Being able to see in the dark
And jump vast distances
And weave a clothes makers web
Skill and expertise incredible

Spider and the lonely prisoner
To become good friends
Talking about world issues for hours
And days in the torturous prison
The spider even letting him
Hold him in awe and amazement
Admiring his acrobatic body

After many miserable months
The prisoner to be released
But never forgetting that magical spider:
A talking spider that helped him cope
And opened up his closed mind
The colourful and vast world now the place
The once prisoner deciding to explore.

Satan's Playground

This used to be my playground
Before the devious devil entered my life
My empty life becoming turbulent
And full of never-ending hassle and stress.

This used to be my playground
Before the ancient battle between
The holy good and the satanic evil
Many involved in the supernatural fight.

This used to be my playground
Before the painful violence began
My life concerned by others
Others questioning my personal choices.

This used to be my playground
Before I lost my innocence
My successful career taking me up and up
My life with money and Irish luck.

This used to be my playground
Before the lashing storm hit
And the world turned to darkness
The sunlight blocked by rainclouds.

This used to be my playground
Before the almighty God intervened
Questioning the doomed devil
Doomed to live in eternal night.

This is still my playground
Now living in the tropical warmth
Of earth I know to be paradise
My wise soul advanced through the years.

Building Castles On The Sand

Fragile and delicate
Moving through life slowly
Emotional wellbeing difficult
Crying endless tears at night
Waking from horrible nightmares in a fright

All alone being developed in a world of tears
No-one being able to help

No matter how nicely you dress it up
Always following the rules nevertheless
Feeling the pain of frustrating poverty

Of always knowing I have less
Of the never-ending stress
That makes the sand sink
With the weight of a strong castle
The sand foundation useless

A perfect day: until the crush
A vast crowd in a rush
Feeling the severe push
Feeling the suffocating crush
Yet no-one really but myself to blame

Feeling bitter and blasphemy
Wondering why God has walked off
And left my strong castle
In the weak and movable sand
The castle now crashing into the sea

My invincible reign ended bitterly
My emotions bent like breeze blocks
Wishing for pointless revenge
Because I should have known better
Than build my indestructible castle on sand.

T-Rex Country: Millions Of Years Ago

Terrifying T-Rex

A dinosaur with a bird brain
A predator causing blood and pain
Its hundred ton body
Making dying dinosaurs
Wince from the bloody pain
Having a heart that could explode
And having bones that could break
If running too fast too soon
Having to protect her young
That hatched from precious dinosaur eggs
Her offspring her job to look after
Steering and scaring away predators
Having no nemesis in the Jurassic forest

Her jaws and teeth capable of crushing
Other dinosaurs her own weight
Her prey necessary to feed her young
Her hunting skills stellar.

Other Dinosaurs

Other dinosaurs ruling the planet
160 million long years
The movie Jurassic Park releasing fears
Dinosaurs to be the Pegomastax
A cross between a parrot and porcupine
A dinosaur not featured in Jurassic Park

Other dinosaurs Velociraptor
Meaning speedy thief
A predator giving other dinosaurs grief
By stealing prey and meat
Leaving other dinosaurs hungry
And searching for easy food.

Types of Therapod Dinosaurs
• Albertosaurus
• Allosaurus
• Baryonyx
• Carnotaurus
• Coelophysis
• Compsognathus
• Deinonychus
• Giganotosaurus
• Megalosaurus
• Ornithomimus
• Oviraptor
• Saurophaganax
• Spinosaurus
• Tyrannosaurus
• Tyrannotitan
• Velociraptor
• Yangchuanosaurus

Therapod dinosaurs waving their short arms
Running with long and powerful legs
Angry when another dinosaur steals their eggs
Chasing the thief, angry with grief
The instinct for survival strong
The ancient world where dinosaurs do belong.

Sauropod Dinosaurs
- Apatosaurus
- Brachiosaurus
- Diplodocus
- Giraffatitan
- Jobaria
- Macrurosaurus
- Mamenchisaurus
- Seismosaurus
- Zigongosaurus

Sauropod Dinosaurs slow
On their four legs
Another type of dinosaur
Protective of their eggs
Few prey for the famous T-Rex
Fear these dinosaurs feel little of

Dinosaur Timeline

Dinosaurs a diverse group of reptiles
Of the clade Dinosauria
Coming into vast existence
The advancing Triassic period
Between 243 and 233.23 million years ago
Humans these dinosaurs never to know

Birds being feathered dinosaurs
Evolving from earlier theropods
The Late Jurassic epoch
Exploding new animals and reptiles
And these dinosaurs dangerous
But long running reptiles

In the early 19th century
First dinosaur fossils were recognized
The name "dinosaur" (meaning "terrible lizard") used
Coined by Sir Richard Owen in 1841
Refer to these "great fossil lizards"
Dinosaurs becoming an enduring part of popular culture

The most famous movie and franchise
"Jurassic Park" first released in 1993
Going on to make millions of dollars
The world mad for dinosaurs

The whole world imagining
Riding on these beasts and bringing them to life

Dinosaur science to populate the media
Scientists learning from fossils
Scientists knowing all types of dinosaurs
And their diets and way of survival
Dinosaurs maybe extinct but still living on
In reptile and other species alive today.

The Singing Poet: Mariah Carey

Mariah Carey born on March 27th 1969
In Huntington New York in the USA
Attending Harborfields High School
Mariah Carey never the fool
In spite of being one of the few mixed race

Mariah Carey street-smart and keeping up the pace
Children and teenager at her school
Racism rife in New York at the time
Yet in later years music and poetry Mariah would entwine
Her music and lyrics to withstand the test of inevitable time

Mariah's parents to be Patricia (née Hickey),
A former opera singer and vocal coach of Irish descent
Alfred Roy Carey, an aeronautical engineer
Of African-American and black Venezuelan-American lineage
Mariah the youngest of three children born to her parents

Mariah's name inspired by "They Call the Wind Maria"
From the 1951 Broadway musical "Paint Your Wagon"
Mariah's surname adopted by her Venezuelan grandfather
Francisco Núñez, after he emigrated to New York
Their family surviving in spite of racial prejudice

Mariah Carey's mother – Patricia –
To be disowned by her family
For daring to fall in love and marry a black man
And even neighbours in Huntington
Poisoned the family dog and set fire to their car

Soon to divorce, a relationship that had its effect and cause
Mariah to lack contact with her father down the line
But her mum to work several jobs with her time

Alison moved in with their father; Mariah and
Her elder brother Morgan lived with their mother

Mariah to grow up and graduate
From Harborfields High School in Greenlawn, New York in 1987
Even though often absent due to demo singing
Mariah already finding a job she was passionate about
A job where she would sing beautiful words instead of shout

Even though nicknamed "mirage" at high school
Mariah completed 500 hours of beauty school
Living in a cramped one bed apartment in Manhattan
Her four female roommates feeling the squeeze
Of lack of money yet wanting to do what they please

Then the Cinderella story came about
Mariah having sang with freestyle Brenda K. Starr
A backup singer and working with
Gavin Christopher and Ben Margulies
A cause and effect that would make Mariah rise to the top

Magically, Mariah to attend a CBS record executives' gala
With Brenda K. Starr and handing her demo tape
To the top man of Columbia Records, Tommy Mottola
The man to find Mariah Carey two weeks later
And the rest is musical history.

Discography
• Mariah Carey (1990)
• Emotions (1991)
• Music Box (1993)
• Merry Christmas (1994)
• Daydream (1995)
• Butterfly (1997)
• Rainbow (1999)
• Glitter (2001)
• Charmbracelet (2002)
• The Emancipation of Mimi (2005)
• E=MC² (2008)
• Memoirs of an Imperfect Angel (2009)
• Merry Christmas II You (2010)
• Me. I Am Mariah... The Elusive Chanteuse (2014)
• Caution (2018)

Mariah Carey to date Tommy Mottola while recording her debut album
They to marry in New York City on the 5th of June 1993

At Saint Thomas Church, the relationship a success but to get worse
Their marriage to end due to Mottola's controlling personality
Their differences separating them on May 30th 1997

But Mariah to meet more attractive men
Her music influenced but the message they'd send
Their personalities not easy to pretend
Once having gotten to know Mariah Carey:
A woman a legend, a career that'll never end

Mariah believing in God: a woman with faith
To often privately pray and in her songs say
That she is a fighter, even when her personal life a mess
And she will pray to God and sometimes confess
Her hard thoughts that are often compressed

Through taking therapy sessions
Medication also helping Mariah's Bipolar II disorder
A condition not uncommon in the population
But a upsetting surprise for Mariah's fans
Who want to help Mariah carry on her musical plans

Mariah breaking sales records throughout her career
Having performed on stage over and over again
With a voice stellar and song writing genius
Mariah Carey shall live forever in people's hearts
And capture the imagination with music that does enchant.

The Scared Scarecrow

An innocent little girl
Being a scared Scarecrow
Hiding in her small bedroom
Wishing the clock would stop
Closing her eyes and wishing she didn't have
To get out of bed and face the world.

An innocent little girl
Being a scared Scarecrow
Keeping her head down low
Hoping not to be noticed
Hoping others cannot see her fears
That are doomed to last years and years.

An innocent little girl

Being a scared Scarecrow
Painfully shy and awkward
Going through teenage years alone
Always wishing she was home
Instead of the packed classroom.

A now attractive self-made young woman
Having made it through the wilderness
Having been shy and quiet
Yet working hard to face people
And survive in the big bad world
Having once been an innocent little girl.

A now daring young woman that she is
Her soul made of yellow straw
Like the Scarecrow in "The Wizard Of Oz"
Unable to be a fearless lion
Wishing for bravery and strength
Wanting to bounce down that yellow brick road,

But people love her deeply
Knowing she is much stronger
For facing all her unsettling fears
Her yellow straw holding her together
In spite of troubles never to fall apart
Because her vulnerabilities shall depart.

I Don't Want To Sleep In The Snow

I don't want to sleep in the pure white snow
Not when I have a beautiful apartment
I don't want to sleep in the cold snow
Not when a comfortable roof over my head
Protects me from the bitter
And incredibly harsh winter snow.

I don't want those snowflakes
Falling upon me in winter darkness
Where my body would freeze
From the harsh winter snow
Those months where nature
Hibernates and waits for colourful springtime.

No matter how pretty and romantic winter
My apartment always protects

Me from winter's cruel coldness
My stylish apartment protects
Me from its supernatural elements
And its enchanting allure.

With all of the people homeless
This bitterly cold winter
You have to pray they find warmth
And give money to homeless charities
Because it could be me:
All it takes is a missed rent payment.

All it takes is an unauthorized
Day off work, your employer
Quick to find a different worker
And you can't afford to be sick
Knowing you don't want to sleep
In the winter on those old church steps.

When Your Cat Scratches You

When your cat scratches you
You know you're in trouble
Do these things come in three?
And you hope your blood you don't see
For an excited cat is a dangerous cat.

Never walk into a tiger or lion enclosure
Knowing big cats beautiful but dangerous
Better to see through a human cage
Perhaps at the New Zealand animal park
Their close-up to big cats experience safe.

Realizing animals beautiful but dangerous
Does perpetually protect humans
From animal encounters and attacks
Although animals have been known
To come to the rescue of people.

Like a pride of strong four lions
Rightfully scaring off a group of men
With unknown reasons attempting to abduct
An innocent six year old girl
But the girl later found safe with her lion saviours.

Other animals known to save human lives
All documented on YouTube videos
Animals to be treasured and protected
Even when the lovely neighbour's cat
Scratches you accidentally in excitement.

And many believe animals to have souls
Animals deeply clever and intuitive
From domestic pets to animals in the wild
And we do take care around any animal
And have a deep respect for their power and allure.

I Don't Want To Sing

I don't want to sing
Even if I had the voice
I wouldn't sing in public
I wouldn't sing in front of friends
I wouldn't sing in front of family
Except for 'Happy Birthday'.

I have no musical talent
I can't play a musical instrument
I can't read or write music
I have no desire to perform music
I have no desire to dance to music
I have no desire to host music shows.

I like watching music videos
But I wouldn't choose to make them
I like listening to pop, rock and jazz albums
But I wouldn't choose to record them
I like watching celebrity interviews on YouTube
But I wouldn't choose to star in them.

I am just your average Joe and Jane
I am just ordinary and anonymous every day
I am just travelling along the busy road
Whether by a private car or busy bus
I have no fame or fortune
And am very happy to be this way.

Stealing From The Thieves

Sitting here listening to Maria McKee sing
"Show Me Heaven"
I wonder where heaven went
Why there is only hell
Criminals playing the game well.

We are only stealing from the thieves
We aren't taking from the innocent
The world vast with its evil
The world vast with its beauty
God the creator a mystery.

We move, we weave, we deceive
We forever wonder and wander
What to buy as our next purchase
Where to travel on that exotic holiday
Private airplanes where we pay over a grand.

We feel relief with every paycheque
We celebrate our never ending wealth
While sending postcards saying "Wish you well"
To our fools: those who dare take from us
And cause us distress and trouble.

We remember the painful trauma
Before our luxurious lives
Sitting in hatred and anger
But now we walk away smug
Knowing we need no drugs.

We attract but repel
We are beautiful but nasty
We are rich but common
We are musical but realistic
We are real but live in fantasy.

Stealing from the thieves
Making us super lucky
Them having no awareness
Of our delight and soul deep happiness
Where they are all invited to my party.

Word Factory

Many words pass through my mind
Words like school shoelaces I must untie
Like upsetting childhood memories
That so forbiddingly unwind

Memories never forgotten
Memories never to change
Memories to sometimes haunt
Memories sometimes simply unwanted

Like a curse words of evil flow
From the depths of the Fire God's
Evil realm not seen from the surface to deep below
Souls haunted and tortured until the burden of chains they tow

Stories written by a servant of the Fire God
Stories written by a servant of the Holy God
Stories written by a servant of the human race
Stories written to show a truly ugly face

I travel from place to place
With memories I shall treasure
Rather than dread or replace
For I am truly beautiful: written upon my face

Sometimes I stop and think
I don't know if I can handle
Dirty dishes in that old kitchen sink
The dining room table also cluttered

But I sit in front of this computer
I write confused and tangled words
My imagination a paradox
Reflected in all my fictional characters

And so the word factory reveals itself
And English Literature does increase my wealth
But I live for stories and people:
People who read my stories with great interest.

An Old Episode Of Star Trek

Watching an old episode of Star Trek
I can only imagine being in space
Even though I have always

Flown on advanced airplanes
Man having once landed on the moon

I don't fear being in the sky
I don't fear being up that high
Thousands of feet up in the air
Sitting on that airplane seat
In comfort and with no care

Watching an old episode of Star Trek
I can only imagine being on the Space Station
Orbiting earth at hundreds of miles per hour
Through the change of day to night
Capturing images of earth in orbit

I don't fear travelling through outer space
I don't fear being up high
Beyond earth's atmosphere
Like a satellite travelling
Through the solar system and beyond

Watching that old episode of Star Trek
I see computers and touch screens
I see mobile talking devices
What we know now as smart phones
Talking across vast distances

Watching that old episode of Star Trek
I see a vision of the future
I see modern and amazing computers
I see NASA searching the Milky Way
I see NASA send satellites into deep space

The human race has reached
The incredible 21st century
We have technology beyond
What we thought we'd need
We have knowledge of science

We have a better understanding:
We know our physics
We know our chemistry
We know our biology
We know our mathematics

Time doesn't stop, the never ending clock

Time moves on constantly like the
Revolving of this beautiful earth
A blue and green fast spinning ball
That forever leaves us to think and recall.

How To Make A Perfect Cup Of Tea

First start with a boiling kettle
Don't let yourself get distracted
Don't let anyone meddle
For you shall be master
Of the sophisticated kettle

Put the teabags into the cup:
Choose a stylish and colourful cup
With various designs from
Modern art to fun cartoons
To even famous mottos sung in songs

Pour the near boiling water
Into the cups of your choice
Making sure your teabags
Are Tetley Tea, PG Tips
Or even the defined Earl Grey

Consider different tea flavours
From fruit teas: to strawberry and raspberry
To herbal teas, such as peppermint tea
Just explore a local tea shop
And think about your tea options

Leave the chosen teabag
To brew for a good three minutes
Then thoroughly stir and pour
Add a dash of milk and some sugar
If you so desire

Your friends and family
Will certainly worship you
For making perfect tea
And your lunch breaks at work
Will never be boring with PG Tips

Because tea is worldwide
Its traditions and social events

Evolve around that cup of tea
People sitting and talking with cake
Together in each other's company

This includes PG Tips
With breakfast
Whether soggy breakfast cereal
Or a well cooked breakfast
Tea always drunk at the start of the day

Tea is served at lunchtime:
With any hot lunch
Enough food to settle the stomach
And stop those hunger pains
That strike when without enough food

Traditional tea to also be made
Of a relaxing evening time
Family sitting around the table
And knowing it'll be bedtime soon
Tea the next day they do correctly assume

So don't let your tea go cold:
Drink it all up and enjoy its lovely taste
Don't let all that effort go to waste
Because tea is an important tradition
And the way people will always bond.

Greek Goddess

Sitting on the beach in a yellow swimsuit
Wearing dark sunglasses
Wearing pale pink lipgloss
Smelling of sunscreen and the sea
Strutting her stuff along the beach
Knowing that heads are turning

Sitting at the cafe in autumn
Dressed in a silver sequinned skirt
Dressed in a purple couture sweater
Covered - yet comfortable and stylish -
In the rain and cooler weather
And dressed in funky black velvet heels

Sitting in the Italian restaurant

At the start of snowy December
Autumn - and autumn rain -
Merely a romantic memory
With all the ghoulish Halloween celebrations
And colourful Guy Fawkes fireworks nostalgic

Sitting around the tree at Christmastime
The Christmas tree sparkling
With electric light jewel colours
Of blue, red, green, yellow, orange, pink and purple
Glittering the Christmas tree like magic
As Christmas presents are excitedly exchanged

Sitting in the busy church at Easter
Springtime glorious like a rainbow
With chocolate bunnies and Easter eggs
Children's faces smeared with milk chocolate
Adults kindly delighting in childhood innocence
Celebrating themselves with red wine in the evening

A Greek Goddess the immortal
Living through life itself
And celebrating in this short, brutal life
Yet magical with its broken dreams
Everyone with some regrets
But life is extraordinary in every way possible.

A Cup Of Coffee

It has been a while: how have you been?
There is so much of the world you must have seen,
I just want your kisses and love: to hear your voice
To talk to you about your adventures:
Where you've been
Your hopes, past loves and secret fears.

How am I? You may ask
Well, I have missed you
And I haven't slept in a while
And for me you'll never go out of fashion
You'll never go out of style
Your personality never dull or repulsive.

How I have missed your beautiful face
And those eyes that I remember so vividly

You always had been my first true love
You never were a fad to me
You'll always reside in this heart
Memories keeping me going when apart.

And I shall go wherever you go
I want to be with you
I want your kiss and your touch
I don't want my heart to be broken
I don't want to be alone in this world
And a broken world it is without you.

You're the only one I can trust
Only you know these deep, inner thoughts
And you'll always be my first and last true love
I look good enough to eat just for you
Because I am crazy for you, so please come along
And have a cup of coffee with me.

We can talk about anything: your life
Your hopes and your dreams
And maybe I can tell you mine
But we'll take things slow
Although I hope never to let you go again
You my first true love and my only real friend.

So I'll see you tomorrow at 11 o'clock in the cafe
I hope you'll be there, so bring only yourself
And leave your mobile phone switched off
Because I have hopes, dreams and fears to share with you
My heart singing a melody, hoping you'll sing along
Where together we can face the world and remain strong.

Eating Dinner At The Table With My T-Rex

Those big, razor sharp teeth,
Those devious, clever eyes,
Those sturdy legs,
That run so fast,
For my T-Rex that hunts,
Is the predator,
Prey captured so quickly,

With dinosaur meat,
So gullible to the silence,

Not realizing evil eyes,
Watching, waiting, hating,
And loving the smells,
Of blood and fear,
My T-Rex with a bird brain,
Quick to chew and swallow,
Feeding on the pain,

And I sit at the dinner table,
With my favourite T-Rex,
A goat's leg for him,
And a juicy steak for me,
And my T-Rex drinks,
A very large cup of blood,
Whereas I drink red wine,
For our meat tastes divine,

Our bloodlust,
Our nature,
Our aggression and determination,
Why we win over prey,
And we always dine together,
And afterwards we cheer,
And make our excuses,
To end an exciting night,

Only to have my T-Rex,
Turn around in his betrayal,
And eat me for dessert.

Forgetting The Perfect House

The newly married couple
Buy the perfect house:
It is in a prime location
It is a four bedroom house
And isn't in a flood area

The neighbours are pleasant
And talk in a friendly tone
The neighbours are welcoming
And nicely enquire
About the married couple

The married couple previously

Lived in a two-bedroom apartment:
An apartment that was too small
Especially with the husband
Being rather tall

Even though the apartment was cosy
It didn't suit their needs
It was cramped and sometimes dusty
Always needed to be aired out
And mould continually removed

So the married couple
Purchased a suburban house
With a busy highstreet nearby
With shops and other amenities
Including a public library and a cosy cafe

At first the new house was spotless
But then real life got in the way
The married couple had to go to work
They had so many bills to pay:
Bills that arrived like clockwork

So the blue carpet wasn't perfectly clean
The bins were not always taken out
But the washing up was done regularly
The laundry washed once a week
Yet still the house became undone

So the married couple hired a cleaner:
Their jobs meant they could afford one
And soon the house became shipshape
They had a clear floor again
And a clear sink every day

They soon realised
They had to forget the perfect house
Their apartment had been easier to clean
But now they live in a home
Where they keep heart and soul.

Apartment Life

I live the apartment life
Where my quiet neighbours

Look through curtained windows
And know all that they can see
But this does not bother me.

I live the apartment life
Going out and about
Where I paint the town red
Boredom when alone indoors at night
Entertainment important to my life.

I live the apartment life
Where I have the perfect interior design:
Peach lounge walls, white bedroom walls
And a gorgeous beige fluffy carpet
My apartment floor soft under the feet.

I live the apartment life
Where my bookshelf contains various items
And my collection of books are showcased
Being a self confessed book lover
Having read famous novels for years.

I live the apartment life
Going to the office every Monday
Having a lie-in every Sunday
For that day is my fun day
And my routine rest day.

I live the apartment life
Eating out and eating in
Cooking for myself with Hello Fresh
But also going out for dinner
Enjoying all the culinary delights.

I live the apartment life
My neighbours also in their apartments
Guests to mine coming and going
Residents coming and going
Month after month, year after year.

I live the apartment life
Airing out the rooms every day
Always washing up and washing the laundry
Always keeping my home pristine
My apartment aesthetically pleasing.

I live the apartment life
Going daily on my computer
Working online as an online legend
And keeping up appearances
Knowing myself a public figure.

I live the apartment life
Inviting fun people over
And serving mostly soft drinks
And just entertaining friends
No one getting drunk however.

I live the apartment life
And will never live in a house:
Because my apartment is home
And I know I am not friendless or alone
For apartment life is my true home.

The Bird That Was Too Afraid To Fly

There once was a bird too afraid to fly
She didn't know how to relate to others
Yet she could never say goodbye
And every night she would cry and cry
For she was a bird too afraid to fly.

She would see others through a computer screen
Every night she would dream and dream
Every nightmare becoming obscene
Yet a nugget of gold
Began to take hold:

She could raise her wings
And soar through paradise
Where everyone knew her and loved her
And need never look twice
Her bird wings taking her through paradise.

And she learnt to believe in herself
She learnt how to gain valuable wealth
She to take her life and steer
At her party she would happily cheer
Knowing her bird wings brought her here:

Here to a never ending paradise

Where magnificent birds take full flight
Through the blue, blue sky
Knowing deeply how and why
They are able to fly,

For they are free
They cure all that is insane
And yet – somehow – make the mad free:
Free to paint colourful rainbows
And view birds soaring through paradise,

Where once fear held her down
Now she does no longer frown
For she is a bird of paradise
Who wears the heavenly kingdom crown
And know what she will always know:

That her wings are vast
That her wings take a chance
And rejoice with hope
And view life with scope
Having once been a bird too afraid to fly.

The Poisoned Cat

Caroline was a kind elderly woman
Who had a soft heart
And a great affection for cats
She would daily feed
Them irresistible Dreamies
Every night and every day

So popular were these cat treats
Cats would venture out
From their cosy homes
Through snow and rain
Across parks and fields
From the weather no shield

To sit inside Caroline's cosy kitchen
Lapping up delicious cream and milk
In clean cat feeding bowls
Enjoying the taste of Dreamies
Enjoying the company of Caroline
Enjoying being content and pampered cats

But what Caroline did not notice
Was the nasty next door neighbour
Looking through her stained net curtains
Feeling jealousy of Caroline's happiness
How she could dare live happily
Shown by Caroline's love of cats

The next day a cat found poisoned
From inside Caroline's once happy home
Her beautiful cats dead
Their empty feeding bowls
Now smelling of cat poison
A villain breaking Caroline's heart

But Caroline would find the cat killer
Caroline would save future cats
Her neighbourhood supporting her
Never ending months going by
And Caroline did still break down and cry
But she cleverly discovered the cat killer

Setting up a devious trap
Caroline caught the bitter old woman
Poisoning a deliberately placed feeding bowl
A feeding bowl no cat to eat or drink from
And the police came for Bitter Billie
Having her held down by police in her rage

With the cat killer behind bars
Caroline returned to entertaining cats
No cat ever poisoned again
Cats loving Caring Caroline
And coming from far and wide
To treasure a nice human on their side.

To A World Beyond The Computer

I don't want to die never seeing the world,
To only sit behind a cold, empty computer,
A computer with no heart or soul,
Where abuse from Twitter spirals out of control,
And Facebook boasts about trips and fake lives,
Inviting strangers into your home,
Cybercrime stealing your details and money,

Just as a pickpocket in the street.

The world beyond a computer goes on,
Because a machine cannot replace life,
For those virtual words can cut,
Just as any aggressive person you might meet,
But getting up in the morning,
Not spending all night on the computer,
And breathing the fresh air,
As you walk down the street,
Is where real street credibility is.

Trains and planes are great places to meet people,
With such a variety of looks and personalities,
And I look to these people with wonder,
Hearing about lives that fascinate,
And adventures a computer cannot replace,
For the world is a vast place,
People to be found in this world,
Not a cold, empty computer.

Computers are useful and important,
But it's the people that count,
Friends to be found in the real world,
As well as the online world,
For this world can be anything and everything,
And you can reach for those famous stars,
Along an adventure called life.

Missing: T-Rex Brought To Life

Jurassic encounter
The children's funfair
Dinosaurs brought to
Realistic robotic life
And made to cause fear
Although excited fear
As the robotic T-Rex comes near

A young Thomas
Waking up that Saturday morning
Never ceasing the yawning
Feels nerves and excitement
Over his cornflakes
Knowing the day is near

And will bring surprises
But poor Thomas
Does not know his fate

Walking into Jurassic encounter
9 year old Thomas
Holding his mother's hand
Gazes around the park in wonder
Amazement at the dinosaurs
From raptors to herbivores
Not all dinosaurs meat eating
Or dinosaurs that hunt

And there are ice cream and candy stalls
There are beautiful plants and flowers
In the vicinity, plus a train
To take visitors around the park
And it was this train
Poor Thomas fell out of
His parents not finding him
Until later that night
But Thomas would now
Have a tale to tell

After failing from the small train
Thomas wandered through the trees
Knowing the train would come back
But not before some important
Lessons were learnt
For Thomas escaped with his life
After encountering a real life T-Rex
Because the robotic dinosaur
Had come to life that evening
And the devil made this so

No one would ever believe
Young Thomas's tale
Being seen as a fantasy
Comparing it to seeing a whale
But he knew hiding and escaping
Had been the right thing to do
After seeing the T-Rex
Wandering around woods
Seemingly searching his new home
No awareness of Thomas

And luckily Thomas kept it that way
Quickly finding the train
And escaping with his life
Because he may never
Have made it out:
Other children not so lucky

For Jurassic encounter
Would see lessons taught
Those evil and malicious eaten by
A robotic T-Rex come to life
Every night on the small train
The guilty to feel pain
The devil teaching lessons
Of those guilty of crimes
And no one to stop this justice
No matter the time period
Because it is all relevant.

Like The T-Rex Said To The Goat

The predator out for the kill
Looking for a quick and powerful thrill
For she is a vicious killer
Enjoying the pain
Enjoying the fear
For she works for the devil
Doing the devil's will
Although never labelled insane
And never being to blame,

And her mind like a T-Rex
Where she leaves her victims perplexed
Her motivation strong
Her motivation pushing others along
For she is the T-Rex and – therefore -
Does no wrong
Even when her victims
Have to be strong
And face the pain that came along
For all victims to be strung along
Games to be vicious, bloody and wrong,

And like the T-Rex said to the goat:
'You've got nothing over me

So why don't you gloat?
I am the T-Rex
And much bigger than you
You should see earlier
The other dinosaurs that flew
As soon as they knew
I was in the vicinity
With my teeth razor sharp
And my legs running fast,

And you – goat –
Are small and weak
And you are so scared
You don't even speak
As I stare down from above you
And know that you will bleed
And be swallowed in pieces
By my urge for raw meat
Knowing the hunger
Knowing the need,

But – goat –
I have some sympathy:
I know I am large
But you can have a head start
As I picture ripping out
Your goat heart
For you are small and insignificant
You matter nothing to me
I just want your blood
And I want your meat
And when I hear your goat screams
I will feast on your body
And remember the delicious taste
Of a goat life not gone to waste,

In my night-time dreams
Knowing I got you to scream
And left you in bloody pieces
The kind that only a T-Rex
Can cause, nightmares
Leaving others terrified
Throughout night-time dreams,
Where you run from me
Hoping to hide and disappear
But all I smell is your fear

And enjoy every moment
As I look at you and get near.'

This is what the T-Rex said to the goat.

Unfeeling Robot

Your heart is made of ice
You have to be asked twice
To be friendly and nice
But your soul cold like ice

You only care about power
You only care about your status
In society and to every stranger
You an evil mortal danger

To others and ultimately yourself
Where you only care about wealth
Your position of power
In society and each violent night hour

You spit on the unlucky poor
But it is you who is really the trash
Your money only borrowed cash
For you have no class

You don't deserve to be happy
You don't deserve wealth
You don't deserve good health
And I will never be there for you

Hope you never sleep in the snow
Hope you never know what I know
Hope you never have to reap what you sow
Hope your life doesn't blow

Psychopath, narcissist or sociopath?
Be honest and tell me which are you?
Hope you never have to choose
From the devil's painful torture chambers

You are an unfeeling robot
Is there any love in your heart?
I hope someone breaks your unfeeling heart

I hope all of Pandora's curses curse you

I shall never be your friend
I will never be there to the end
You I truly hate and truly loathe
And I hate everything about you

Never ask me for money:
You are on your own
So don't come begging
When broke: you're alone

I hope you love yourself:
Because I certainly don't
And other insults in my mind
Making me want to gloat.

Distortion On My Headphones

Whispering in my ears
Music playing on my headphones
No matter the genre of music
From rock, pop to dance
Disguising the inner voices
My mind tricking me
With predictions of the future
And money that will never arrive
Unlike those stars that survive
Every song taking its stance

Voice heard on a tape
'Watch how she hurts'
Some kind of demon setting to work
To destroy my flamboyant life
Of worth and mirth
Centuries spent on this earth
Songs always played for a happy life

Myself an unwritten immortal
A soul to survive hell on earth
With every kind of drama
Even those in nightclubs
And every wound inflicted
My body remembering the upset
Incessant voices in my mind

Like a lashing school cane
Music on my headphones making me sane

The past my torment
The present my choice
The future my fate
Where tears roll down my face
When I thought I could relate
And not live in a world made of hate
Distortion on my headphones
Making it pour with rain

But people with their own opinions
People with their own problems
People with their own issues
Issues I knew no knowledge of
The world seemingly without love
I only knowing the angels above

And every night, every moment,
Every day, week, month and year
Add up to millions of tears
Where all I ever find
Is paralysing and soul destroying fear
Knowing it doesn't matter the year
Playing my music at night
My headphones disguising
My problematic life

The distortion on my headphones also
Distracting my vicious thoughts
Images of satisfying revenge
That only torture me
But in the world I see
How I can learn to be free
Knowing music on my headphones
Brings me home

Those old whispers in my mind
Trying to make me unkind
Yet I see the signs
Of the route I must go
To free me from these chains
Myself always taking the blame
A scapegoat living with the shame

But I no longer feel that shame
Because for your crimes
Only you will ultimately pay
As I listen to my music
My headphones distorting the pain
My soul happy today.

Terminator: War Of The Robots

The earth year 3000
Terminator the 1984 graphic film
Robots on the rampage
War after devastating war
Sabotage of the robots

Developed early
In primitive yet advanced
Technology moving forward
Century after century
Even ancient Rome to the Victorians
To carry the story of technology
Scientists and philosophers
With their vast imagination
Of the galactic future

For Sophia the robot
The first real robot
To learn the English language
To learn human movement
And to communicate efficiently
The robot an attractive humanoid

Although other robots
Functional yet basic
Theory of technology
Advancing this modern world
Taking humans to the 21st century
Making the legends' predictions come true
Psychic visions of technology
Pulling humankind into virtual reality

Where they travel through space
NASA sending the Rover robot
To Mars, the red planet
That has always fascinated

Humans when the planet discovered
Centuries ago by astronomers

And robots walk and talk
That even deliver mail
Their futuristic programming
Highly advanced
Yet totally simple
When scientifically applied
To technological theories

And computers are able
Talk to all people in any language
Like the speaker Alexia
Google to be innovative
With their clever applications

Earth year 3000 comes around
Robots with threatening intelligence
Racing for the destruction that is war
Able to drive the car in any situation
Themselves to shoot guns
Navigate geographical areas
Turn lights on and off in homes
Lock doors
Set off alarms
And make terrible trouble

But will robots
Destroy humankind?
Or will humans
Destroy themselves
With their own guns
And own crimes
Against humanity?

We must save ourselves
No matter the robots
We create and control
With our knowledge
Of computer science
And other subjects
In science and technology
That benefit this planet

Where our destiny lies

Only we can decide
And keeping control
Will save our planet
Every time we protect
Our fellow citizens

No matter the century
We are the masters
Of destiny and fate
And only the human race
Can stop the soul destroying hate.

Deep Space Exploration

From the mission to Mars
To the mysteries of deep space
Dark matter and dark energy
The complex works
The universe does
Where negative versus positive
The universe a paradox in itself

Opposites making explosions
Making moons and planets
To either be in unstoppable heat
Or freezing cold temperatures
Impossible for man to land on
Only to be able to view
From lenses of cameras
And views from satellites

In deep space spaceships
Send the public to the moon
And to the mission of Mars
And to planets in the solar system
Planets and moons
Circulating like blood in veins
Once deep space seen
The soul to never be the same

NASA space station orbiting earth
Another NASA space station
Orbiting the red planet Mars
That old planet desolate of life
Earth the only planet to harvest life

No matter the trouble and strife
Of maintaining flourishing life

The cost of space travel not vast
Safety paramount
When dressed in
Space issue attire and a mask
For reaching across the universe
To be the goal of NASA
And other space agencies

Pilots to count and measure
Seconds, minutes and hours
The spaceship going
In four dimensions:
Up and down
Left and right
Even female pilots to do the job
Keeping the spaceship in gear
From flying airplanes
To going into deep space
Where they take charge and steer

For the space age is now officially here.

An Old Typewriter

I remember my old typewriter:
I used to write my stories on it,
And I would create and build new worlds with words.
This was before computers, of course,
And I still have those stories, for I am very creative,
I have to be as I've read a lot,
And have a vast imagination,
And how I loved sitting there, typing away,
For this may have been yesterday, but it was real,
And my work has proved popular,
For I would type away and within a few hours,
I'd have a hundred or so pages of the printed word,
For I had a voice that wanted to be heard,
And I don't regret those hours spent at the typewriter,
Because, even today, people are reading my work,
Writing is much the same process as it was back then,
It's just a case of hammering at the keys,
And letting one's muse take control,

A bit like a pianist or violinist at their instrument,
But it isn't the actual instrument that matters:
It is how you play it, and words may be words,
But it is the order they are in,
The way they are put together,
It all has to be aesthetically pleasing and easy to read,
And a little imagination goes a very long way,
For there is more to a love story than a broken heart,
There is more to a crime thriller than a few gun shots,
It is a case of adding a love interest,
And a gangster with a conscience.
And you can write about Christmas and Easter,
Telling of whatever takes your fancy,
About these celebratory seasons,
And you could write of ghosts and goblins in the woods at night,
It is all relative, and all areas can be explored,
There are worlds within worlds, there're real life people,
And characters,
And it doesn't matter whether it is explored,
At a computer screen, or years back at a typewriter:
It is about designing a world; designing a story,
Inside your own brain, your mind your instrument.

Scorpio Rising

In the dark of the night,
The moon of Scorpio rises,
Spaceships fly to Mars,
Man the God of the stars,
Venus shines her beauty,
While Pluto stays cold,
And the heat of the sun,
Burns metal into gold,
An array of stars,
Twinkle in the Milky Way,
Other galaxies a realm,
Of man's space travel dreams,
But where to find God,
They do not know,
Only the light of the moon,
To be seen in Earth's shadow,
For darkness shows,
The light of the stars,
Many colours shining,
Like the colours of the rainbow.

Space revellers party on Mars,
While Earth's scrap and waste,
Sent to burn in the sun,
While space police,
Watch the pirates,
That have travelled with NASA,
To the glory of the stars,
And wars are waged,
In the galaxy of the Milky Way,
While spacemen search for life:
Another Earth to inhabit,
Earth seemingly burning in the fumes,
Of rockets and nuclear bombs,
The people have tried to stop,
But Earth regenerates,
Trees grow back,
To their former glory,
Plants releasing oxygen,
Into the cleansed atmosphere,
And the moon lights,
The skies of the night,
Time to continue on,
Man busy with space,
And all of the adventures it offers,
His greatest treasure,
Really the earth he's leaving behind,
The moon of Scorpio rising.

Leo roars with power and strength.
Virgo will see the truth but can be rigid.
Libra balances the scales with diplomacy and grace.
Scorpio stings with spite,
Though you may never know.
Sagittarius throws the arrow into the heart,
And laughs with a sunshine smile.
Capricorn pushes with his horns,
Working hard to get his way,
And being loyal to the end.
Aquarius is quirky and cool,
But can be stubborn and aloof.
Pisces swims with the mermaids,
But can never decide which way to go.
Aries is the fiery ram that goes for the kill.
Taurus is the stubborn ox down to earth and practical.
Gemini is the twin that can see both sides,

But join as one.
While Cancer is the crab that moves with the tide,
And is soft and sensitive:
The water sign that lives off emotion.

Xaviere: Robot By Female Design

The robot made in Earth Year 3000,
Named the original name Xaviere,
A robot by female design,
By those engineers and scientists,
With their contracts to sign.

A robot pretty,
As she is functional,
Xaviere the modern name,
Her tasks to be decided,
Xaviere able to talk,
And talk quickly,
And she also does more than walk:
A robot able to carry out human tasks,
For Xaviere never becomes sickly,
Never gets tired, never gets bored,

Tasks always done,
Tasks never ignored,
And her eyes see the sun,
Even though a robot;
For her programming,
Works 24/7
Making the work place,
Easier to work in,
Work a lighter load,
And objects Xaviere does load,
For fewer work accidents,
And stress to unload,
For human workers,
And she works the hours,
From seven to eleven,
Even cracking secret codes,
When needed.

Xaviere a beautiful robot,
With sapphire eyes,
A roman nose,

And a perfect smile,
For she is made by female design,
The contract they did sign,
Xaviere worth millions,
The second of her kind,
After Sophia the robot,
Who knows the English language,
And is never able to be unkind,
And has eyes that are never blind,

For these robots are beautiful,
Unique, aesthetically pleasing,
With their appearance,
And highly intelligent machines,
That walk and talk,
Never with human emotions,
Like fear, rage, jealousy,
Hate and any other emotion,
But she does not feel love,
Whereas most humans do,
And Xaviere asks about this,
And asks how it feels to kiss,
But a robot does not know,
And will never know,
How love goes,
Although beautiful robots,
By female design.

Xaviere programming,
To be highly advanced,
No function left to chance,
Whether intellectual or physical,
For she is able to lift,
And carry heavy objects,
She is able to write words,
And solve complicated,
Mathematical equations,
She has that ability,
And her English stellar,
Her robot brain records words,
And can also record music,
That is being played on a stereo,

Xaviere built with care and love,
Even though she does not feel love,
Or other human emotions,

But this makes her fearless,
Able to do dangerous work,
And her programming,
Means she has the upper hand,
In the place of work,
Knowledge she does understand,
Her invention in demand,
Robots essential in industry,
And robots who carry the weight,
Without knowing their responsibility,
Nothing to hurt human hands.

Child Of The Universe

I am a child of the universe,
I see into the future,
I see into the past,
And know that this time won't last,
Time rapidly moving,
Time never to stop.

I see the earth in orbit,
I see galaxies and solar systems,
Speeding along their way,
The universe a vast place,
Time rippling through time and space.

Dark matter and black holes,
Time ripples through,
Space and time,
Light never in a straight line,
And gravity distorting time,
Earth's clock not in a straight line,
When travelling across the stars,

Spaceships take us to Mars,
Man now conquering the stars,
For pulsar stars shine rapid light,
While black holes take it from sight.

Planets spin in orbit,
The sun burning into unstoppable heat,
Moons and planets hostile places,
In the not empty space,
Dark matter and dark energy,

The reason the universe sticks like glue.

Satellites travel to distant stars,
Measuring light,
And helping the mission to Mars,
For man is god of the stars.

I am a child of the universe,
I am psychic and know the world,
For I see through God's eyes,
Into a universe of magic and surprise,
Knowledge of space science,
Increasing with every year,
Astronomers, astrophysicists,
And every other type of scientist,
To uncover secrets of the universe,
And invent technology,
Man conquering space,
And man living beyond life of the earth,
An earth four billion years old,
And counting,
The dinosaurs long since gone,
And man now the boss.

Blue Candy

Dots of light scatter across the view,
From a distance I'm closer to the view.
The water moves as the boats remain silent in the view,
The screams from the park sheltered by the moon.
Blue firemen spread their heat,
The powder now a liquid with emotions to defeat.
People fire their souls as the rides end their attack,
Blue candy waiting inside them to react.

I travel along the water through my mind's eye,
Remembering myself with blue candy's tie.
I look to the park: distanced from the view,
The view ending with my eyes looking to the moon.
I see no clouds as the fire spreads inside,
Desire blue candy hitting in all minds,
Raw emotion no longer hidden inside.

Blue candy burns inside my mind,
The powder waiting to leave my past behind.

Blue candy fires as it heats like the sun:
Once inside it cannot be undone.
Every line is stirred under a darkened moon,
Burning desire blue candy's monsoon.
Like fire I call blue candy to defeat,
I lying alone in a city's white light heat.

Albert Einstein

Albert Einstein born 14th of March 1879,
Ulm, the Kingdom of Wurttemberg, German Empire,
Having lived in life, places such as Italy,
Switzerland, Belgium and the United States,
A man always interested in his education,
A man fascinated by science,
All the information he could know and see,
Following into physics and quantum mechanics,
And also to have influence in the philosophy of science,

To think near the beginning of his career,
That Newtonian mechanics,
No longer able to reconcile with laws,
Of the electromagnetic field,
Leading Albert Einstein to,
Publish a paper on special theory of relativity,
Another paper to be published,
On the subject of general relativity,
The year 1916, and including,
Statistical mechanics and thermal,
Properties of light to lay down,
The foundation of the photon theory of light,
Other scientists to not be able,
To disagree and put up a fight,

Albert living in Switzerland between 1895 - 1914,
Bar one year in Prague,
And achieving a academic diploma,
From the Swiss polytechnic school,
The other students to realize him not a fool,
For he went onto being awarded a PhD,
The University of Zurich,
Making a legend happen,
Albert Einstein to turn the key,
Into the exciting world of science,

Adolf Hitler crossing paths with Albert Einstein,
Einstein not to return to Germany,
With his Jewish background,
Presenting a risk to his life,
For going there would be playing with a die,
But Albert Einstein had bigger fish to fry,

For Albert Einstein endorsed a letter,
To President Franklin D. Roosevelt,
Claiming the potential development,
Of "extremely powerful bombs of a new type"
This discovery of warfare to destroy lives,
But the Eve of World War 2 on the cards,
And America wanted to be great,
Even if that meant to destroy,
Rather than create,

But Einstein also to denounce,
The idea of using nuclear fission as a weapon,
The good man knowing the danger,
British philosopher Bertrand Russell,
Working with him to stop the bombs,
But bombs that are still here today,
No one wanting the third world war to come,
Political matters to arise,
Conflict to happen, war never a surprise.

Albert Einstein publishing over 300 scientific papers,
Not being read by those time wasters,
With no skill at science and no interest,
In furthering knowledge and technology,
But Albert Einstein changed the world,
The world knowing his name,
Even after his death in 1955,
The world celebrates him,
The genius and wonderful,
Man and scientist that he will always be,
Theories the world to measure and see,
Just how far we can move humanity.

Paradox

I am a thief, yet I am a giver,
I am a psychopath, yet I am an empath,
I tell horror stories, yet I tell happy stories,

I am the devil, yet I am god,
I am a demon, yet I am an angel,
I kill, yet I save,
I am dark, yet I am light,
I am a liar, yet I am truthful,
I am a coward, yet I am a hero,
I am an actor, yet I am real,
I steal riches, yet make those rich,
I am a stone, yet I am a diamond,
I am poor, yet I am rich,
I am fire, yet I am water,
I am dust, yet I am alive,
I am dead, yet I am born,
I lack desire, yet I create desire,
I put some into hell, yet take those into heaven,
I am dirty, yet I am clean,
I feel hate, yet I feel love,
I am religious, yet I have no religion,
I abandon, yet I comfort,
I am nothing, yet I am all there is,
I am the end of time, yet start time,
I am female, yet I am male,
I am poison, yet I am medicine,
I make some cold, yet give warmth,
I am hot, yet I am cold,
I am shy, yet I am bold,
I am young, yet I am old,
I am the snow, yet I am the sun,
I have lost, yet I have won.

I am wrong, yet I am right,
I am black, yet I am white,
I am nice, yet I am nasty,
I create, yet I destroy,
I am positive, yet I am negative,
I am asleep, yet I am awake,
I am blind, yet I can see,
I am deaf, yet I can hear,
I am silent, yet I have a voice,
I am aggressive, yet I am passive,
I am chaos, yet I am order,
I am confused, yet I am clear-headed,
I am hardworking, yet I am lazy,
I am a dreamer, yet I am practical,
I am ugly, yet I am beautiful,
I am slow, yet I am fast,

I am sweet, yet I am sour,
I am night, yet I am day,
I am queen, yet I am king,
I am a joker, yet I am a fool,
I am a birthday, yet I am a funeral.

I am the paradox.

THE END

2023

www.ingramcontent.com/pod-product-compliance
Lightning Source LLC
Chambersburg PA
CBHW081057170526
45166CB00006B/2097